Y0-BUB-377

FIFTEENTH CENTURY BIBLES.

Fifteenth Century Bibles

A

STUDY IN BIBLIOGRAPHY

BY

WENDELL PRIME

LONGWOOD PRESS
BOSTON

Library of Congress Cataloging in Publication Data

Prime, George Wendell, 1837-1907.
    Fifteenth century Bibles.

    Reprint of the 1888 ed. published by A. D. F.
Randolph, New York.
    1. Bible--Bibliography. 2. Incunabula--Bibliog-
raphy. I. Title.
[Z7770.P85 1977]   [BS1]   016.2204   77-85626
ISBN 0-89341-320-8

Published in 1977 by LONGWOOD PRESS INC.
P.O. Box 535, Boston, Massachusetts 02148

This Longwood Press book is an unabridged
republication of the edition of 1888.
Library of Congress Catalogue Card Number: 77-85626
International Standard Book Number: 0-89341-320-8

Printed in the United States of America

To the Reader:

Many who have a genuine regard for old and good books have not made the acquaintance of those books which are both the oldest and best of printed volumes. This study of the Bibles of the Fifteenth Century includes the oldest of printed books, and only those which are included in the class called INCUNABULA, namely, books printed during the first half-century of the art, 1450=1500, A. D. Thus the history of the printed Bible is the history of the invention and progress of the art of printing.

Wendell Prime.

CHAPTER I.

*

Ƭ𝔥𝔢 𝔅𝔦𝔟𝔩𝔦𝔠𝔞𝔩 𝔎𝔦𝔫𝔤𝔡𝔬𝔪.

THE FIRST BOOK IS THE BIBLE. It is the first complete book which was printed with movable types. It is the first book in the number of its editions, copies and translations. In this respect it exceeds every other book so immensely that there is no other book with which it may be compared. Considered entirely apart from its contents, character and claims, it is easily the first book, standing alone among books of all languages, nations and ages.

The first book printed with movable types was printed by John Gutenberg at Mentz, Germany, between 1450 and 1456 A. D. This claim to be the Alpha of all printed books, as it is daily the Omega of all printed books, has been disputed with all possible ingenuity and erudition. But no other volume, up to the present hour, has found any recognition as its predecessor. Holland makes the most persistent and plausible rival claim to the invention of printing. If Laurens Janszoon Coster of Haarlem should ever be acknowledged as an earlier printer than Gutenberg, which is not at all probable, this would not in the least degree affect the position of THE GUTENBERG BIBLE AS THE FIRST BOOK in the annals of Typography.

It is considered the most splendid specimen of typography extant. Like the sculpture of Phidias, it sprang into being, without a predecessor, in defiance of the theory of evolution. Its successors number, it may be, 250,000,000. No one need dispute about these figures, for more Bibles are now printed daily, than at any previous period, and therefore every day adds to their number by thousands. No other book ever influenced men to bestow their treasures of time, learning and money to print, publish and send it forth by millions. There are Shakespeare Societies and Browning Societies, but their sphere is comparatively narrow and insignificant. All endeavors of every kind to exalt or disseminate published writings serve to show that the Bible as a successful book has no peer. All other books follow at so vast a distance that it shines alone, a sun among the planets. The Bible is the only book for which languages are invented that it may be multiplied in regions where written and printed words were previously unknown.

Astronomers endeavor to aid us in our conception of stellar distances by comparing them with the greatest terrestrial distances with which we are familiar. By similar comparison we may obtain some conception of the vastness of the Biblical sphere compared with that of the most popular of all other publications. The world has produced less than six books which have been translated into thirty or forty languages and whose editions can be counted by a few hundreds. But the Bible has been translated into more than 200 languages, and many years ago its known editions were at least 30,000.

It is believed by those who have devoted the most attention to bibliography that Thomas-à-Kempis's

𝕴𝖒𝖎𝖙𝖆𝖙𝖎𝖔𝖓 𝖔𝖋 𝕮𝖍𝖗𝖎𝖘𝖙

ranks next to the Bible in the number of its editions, translations and copies. It was first printed at Augsburg, by Günther Zainer, in 1468, a small folio of seventy-six leaves, and was reprinted more than twenty times before the end of the century. But before the end of this same century nearly a thousand editions of the Bible had been issued. In 1864, the late celebrated bibliographer, Augustine de Backer, published a bibliographical "Essai" on the "Imitation" in which he enumerated about three thousand editions. Before his death, in 1873, he had collected evidence of more than three thousand additional editions. His learned brother, Aloys de Backer, took up his brother's work, and was preparing a second edition of the "Essai," inclusive of still more editions, when death ended his labors in 1883. In 1838, a collection of different editions of the "Imitation"

was given to the municipal library of Cologne which
contained 400 copies.

The Pilgrim's Progress,

by John Bunyan, probably ranks next to the "Imitation"
in the number of its editions, translations and copies.
The first part was first printed in London, 1678, a copy
of which is in the Lenox Library.   In the Bunyan
collection in this library there are 278 editions of the
first part, 196 of the second part, and 73 of the third
part.

Don Quixote,

by Cervantes, is probably the third most popular book
ever printed.   Its first part was first printed at Madrid,
1605, and its second part was first printed in the same
place 1612.   It has been translated into all European
languages, including Turkish and Greek, and several
times in all the leading languages.   About 300 editions
are known, only one-third of which were printed in
Spain.

It is not probable that there is a fourth book in any
language which approaches any one of these three
mentioned, in the number of its copies, translations and
editions.   Whatever may be the circulation of these or
any other world-famous books, none has been or is so
successful as to alter the relative position of the Bible
in the world of printing, for its editions are numbered
by the tens of thousands, and its translations by the

hundreds.   Practically, its editions are innumerable because it has been printed in so vast a variety of forms. These different forms and issues could not be estimated with any approach to accuracy unless several persons in every generation were devoted to this one biblio-graphical endeavor.   Doubtless the majority of these editions have in their number of copies averaged larger than the ordinary editions of other books, and this adds greatly to its relative supremacy.

In this numerical comparison the Koran is not forgotten.   Though it is read or heard by the millions of Islam, its character and usage remove it from the category in which the Bible is considered.   It is among reading, printing, progressive nations that the Bible is the first book, the "Book of Books," every year more and more without a rival.   This Biblical conquest seems more marvelous when we consider that it has been achieved, in spite of the deadly hostility of what was known throughout the world as Christianity, when printing was invented.

CHAPTER II.

❋

Ⓣ𝔥𝔢 𝔅𝔦𝔟𝔩𝔦𝔠𝔞𝔩 ℭ𝔬𝔫𝔣𝔩𝔦𝔠𝔱.

M UCH is written, especially by scientists, about the conflict between science and religion. Science ought not to complain. Its conflict is a mere lover's quarrel compared with the conflict of the Bible with religion. This entire book, closely printed, would not suffice for a record of the bulls, canons, edicts, confiscations, imprisonments, tortures, stranglings, burnings and other ecclesiastical demonstrations to suppress and exterminate the Bible, its translators, editors, printers, publishers, disseminators and readers. Pagan Rome was not more ferocious in her endeavor to obliterate the Gospel than papal Rome in her attempt to exterminate the Scriptures.

This conflict of the printed Bible was inevitable in view of the position occupied by the Church of Rome for several centuries. We record briefly a few of the most significant incidents in this most tragical chapter in the annals of bibliography.

In 1080, Uratislaus, the King of Bohemia, asked Hildebrand if he might have the offices, or prayers of the church, performed in the SLAVONIAN tongue, at that time the common language of the north of Europe. To this the Pontiff replied: "I will never consent for services to be performed in the Slavonian tongue. *It is the will of God that his word should be hidden, lest it should be despised if read by every one;* and if, in condescension to the weakness of the people, the contrary has been permitted, it is a fault which ought to be corrected. The demand of your subjects is imprudent; I shall oppose it with the authority of St. Peter; and you ought, for the glory of God, to resist it with all your power."

In 1229, the Council of Toulouse, held by Romanus, Cardinal of St. Angelo, and the Pope's legate, formed the *first courts of Inquisition*, and published the *first canon which forbade the Scriptures to the laity.* Forty-five canons were passed by this Council of Toulouse for the extinction of heresy, and the very first of them all forbade the laity to possess any of the books of the Old or New Testaments except, perhaps, the Psalter. Having any of these translated into the vulgar tongue was strictly forbidden. This same Council established the Inquisition by the decree which erected in every city a Council of Inquisitors, and thus the papal condemnation of the Bible is forever associated with the most infamous judicial horror which has disgraced humanity.

The canon prohibiting the Scriptures is in the following terms :—

> *Prohibemus etiam, ne libros Veteris Testamenti aut Laici permittantur habere : nisi forte Psalterium, vel breviarium pro divinis officis, aut Horas Beatæ Mariæ, aliquis ex devotione habere velit, sed ne præmissos libros habeant in vulgari translatos, arctissime inhibemus.*

"We also forbid the laity to possess any of the books of the Old or New Testaments, except perhaps some one out of devotion wishes to have the Psalter or Breviary for the divine offices, or the Hours of the Blessed Virgin. But we strictly forbid them having any of these books translated into the vulgar tongue." *

In the middle of the fifteenth century, lightnings flashed from Gutenberg's printing-press in Mentz. Thunders soon followed from the palaces of priests. Though at first welcoming the new and wonderful art as an aid and ally, they soon discovered its real significance and power. Berthold, Archbishop of Mentz, in 1486, issued an edict forbidding the printing of any religious book in German without permission from ecclesiastical

---

* See LABBEI, *Sacro-Sancta Concilia*, tome ii., pt. i., p. 430.

authority. Before the date of this edict, there were laws in regard to the censorship of books and instances of books printed by permission. But the oldest mandate, appointing a *Book-censor*, with which we are acquainted, is that issued by Berthold, Archbishop of Mentz, in the year 1486, which the curious reader will not be displeased to see at full length, in an English version, with the Instructions given to the censors :—

> *Penal Mandate, forbidding the Translation into the Vulgar Tongue, etc., of Greek, Latin, and other Books, without the previous approbation of the doctors, etc.*

" BERTHOLD, by the grace of God, Archbishop of the Holy See of Mentz, arch-chancellor of Germany, and electoral Prince of the Holy Roman Empire."

" ALTHOUGH, by a certain divine art of printing, abundant and easy access is obtained to books on every science necessary to the attainment of human learning; yet we have perceived that certain men, led by the desire of vain-glory, or money, do abuse this art; and that what was given for the instruction of human life is perverted to purposes of mischief and calumny. For, to the dishonoring of religion, we have seen in the hands of the vulgar certain books of the divine offices, and writings of our religion, translated from the Latin into the German tongue. And what shall we say of the sacred laws and canons, which, though they have been written in the most suitable and careful manner by men acquainted with law, and endowed with the greatest skill and eloquence, yet the science itself is so intricate, that the utmost extent of the life of the wisest and most eloquent man is scarcely equal to it? Some volumes on this subject certain rash and unlearned simpletons have dared to translate into the vulgar tongue, whose translation, many persons who have seen it, and those, too, learned men, have declared to be unintelligible, in consequence of the very great misapplication and abuse of words. Or, what is to be said of works on the other sciences, with which they sometimes even intermingle things that are false; and which, in order the more readily to find purchasers for them, ' they inscribe with false titles, and attribute to notable authors what are merely their own productions?' "

"Let such translators, whether they do this with a good or with a bad intention, let them, if they pay any regard to truth, say whether the German tongue be capable of expressing that which excellent writers, both Greek and Latin, have most accurately and argumentatively written on the sublime speculations of the Christian religion, and on the knowledge of things. They must acknowledge that the poverty of our idiom renders it insufficient; and that it will be necessary for them to invent, from their own minds, new terms for things; or that, supposing them to make use only of the old ones, they must corrupt the sense of the truth, which, from the greatness of the danger attendant upon it, in the sacred writings, we greatly dread; for who would leave it to ignorant and unlearned men, and to the female sex, into whose hands copies of the Scriptures may have fallen, to find out the true meaning of them? · For instance, let the text of the Holy Gospels, or of St. Paul's Epistles, be examined, and no one of any knowledge will deny that there is a necessity for many things to be supplied, or understood, from other writings."

" These things have occurred to our minds, because they are the most common.   But, what shall we think of those which are pending in very sharp disputes among writers in the Catholic Church?   Many other instances might be brought forward, but it is sufficient for our purpose to have named a few."

" But, since the beginning of this art arose *divinely* (to give it its proper appellation) in this our golden city of Mentz, and continues in it to this day in its most improved and perfect state, it is with the greatest justice that we defend the glory of the art, and it becomes our duty to preserve the unspotted purity of the divine writings.   Wherefore, with a view of meeting and restraining, as with a bridle, the aforesaid errors, and the daring attempts of shameless or wicked men, as far as we are able by the will of God, whose cause is in question :—we do, by strictly charging the observance of these presents, command all and every the ecclesiastical and secular persons subject to our jurisdiction, or transacting business within its limits, of whatever degree, order, profession, dignity, or condition they may be, that they translate no works on any science, art, or

knowledge, whatsoever, from the Greek, Latin, or other
language, into the vulgar German; nor, when translated,
either dispose of, or obtain copies, publicly or privately,
directly or indirectly, by any kind of barter, unless
before their impression they shall have been admitted,
by patent, to be sold, by the most noble and honourable
our beloved Doctors and Masters of the University in
our City of Mentz, JOHN BERTRAM DE NUREMBERG,
in *Theology;* ALEXANDER DIETHRICH, in *Law;* THEO-
DORIC DE MESCHEDE, in *Medicine;* and ALEXANDER
ELER, in *Arts;*—the Doctors and Masters deputed for
this purpose in the University of our City of Erfurt; or
if in the town of Frankfurt, the books exposed for sale
shall have been seen and approved by an honourable,
devout, and beloved master in theology, belonging to
the place, and one or two Doctors and Licentiates,
annually paid for that purpose by the Governor of the
said town. And whoever shall treat with contempt this
our provision, or shall lend his counsel, assistance, or
favor, in any way, directly or indirectly, in opposition to
this our mandate, let him know that he has by so doing
incurred the sentence of excommunication; and besides
the loss of books exposed for sale, a penalty of one
hundred florins of gold, to be paid into our treasury;
from which sentence none may absolve him without
special authority."

"Given at the chancery of St. Martin, in our City of
Mentz, under our seal, on the Fourth day of the month
January, MCCCCLXXXVI."

The following are the "*Instructions*" issued to the Censors, and accompanying this Mandate :—

"BERTHOLD, etc., to the honourable, most learned, and beloved in Christ, JO. BERTRAM, doctor in *Theology ;* AL. DIETHRICH, doctor in *Law ;* TH. DE MESCHEDE, doctor in *Medicine;* and AL. ELER, master of *Arts ;*— Health, and attention to the things underwritten."

"Having found out several scandals and frauds, committed by certain translators of literary works and printers of Books, and wishing to counteract them, and according to our power to block up their way, we command that no one in our diocess, or under our jurisdiction, translate any books into the German tongue, or print, or sell them when printed, unless, in our City of Mentz, such works or books have first, according to the form of the *mandate* above published, been by you seen, and as to their matter approved of, both for translation and for sale."

"We do, therefore, by the tenor of these presents, (having great confidence in your prudence and circumspection), charge you, that if at any time, any works, or Books, intended to be translated, printed, or sold, be brought to you, you shall weigh their matter, and, if they cannot be easily translated according to the true sense, but would rather beget errors and offences, or be injurious to modesty, you shall reject them ; and whatever Books you shall judge worthy to be allowed, two of you, at least, shall sign them at the end, with your own hand, in order that it may more readily appear what Books have been seen and allowed by you. In so doing you will perform an office pleasing to our God, and useful to the state."

"Given at the chancery of St. Martin, under our privy seal, the Tenth of January, MCCCCLXXXVI." *

What the Council of Trent did in the middle of the sixteenth century to prevent the knowledge of the Bible is too well known to repeat at length. Its prohibitions were as humorous as numerous. Pious scholars were not allowed to read versions of the Old Testament made by heretics unless they obtained permission of the Bishop. No scholar, however pious, was allowed to read such versions of the New Testament. As vernacular versions were not made and multiplied except by heretics, of course all this was meant to be prohibitory.

William Tyndale, after years of secret translating and printing, was caught in Antwerp, strangled and burned in the prison yard of the castle of Vilvorden, October 6th, 1536. His New Testaments were burned in the public squares of Antwerp and London.

John Rogers edited, revised and prepared for the press the folio Bible known as Matthew's Bible, 1537. He was burned alive at Smithfield in the presence of his wife and eleven children — Queen Mary's first victim.

---

* See BECKMANN'S *Hist. of Inventions*, vol. iiii., pp. 108-113, for the Latin; where, also, reference is given to GUDEN's *Codex Diplomaticus*, tome vi.

Nothing less than a translator or editor of the Bible was worthy of such glory, honor and immortality.

Thirty years after the invention of printing, the Inquisition was in completely successful operation in Spain. Of 342,000 persons punished by it in that country 32,000 were burned alive. It was the Bible which brought them to the flames of martyrdom. Equally terrible was this engine of destruction in Italy, both at the north and south. Archbishops, aided by the Inquisition, were consuming fires for both Bibles and their readers. Nero made some Christians shine as lights in the world by setting them on fire, sewed up in sacks, covered with pitch, using them as candles to illuminate the scene of his debaucheries. But the streets of European cities blazed with Bible bonfires. Bibles were not like readers who could be impoverished, stripped, tortured, mutilated and cast out. Even a leaf surviving might pierce the blackness of this darkness like a star. Just as to the Western frontier men there were no good Indians but dead Indians, so to terrified ecclesiastics there were no good Bibles but burnt Bibles. These holy fires had been far more frequent and brilliant but for the lack of fuel. In many places there were no Bible bonfires merely because authority was so vigilant that there were no Bibles to burn. Bibles were preserved by being carried away by exiles, or by being concealed like precious stones and metals in times of distress and danger.

This fury was not local and political, peculiar to

some place or nation. Robert Stephens, the prince of
French printers, though shielded by King Francis,
could not escape prosecution, ruin and exile for his
Bibles of 1545 and 1549. Generations later, even in
France, the Bible fared no better. Pasquier Quesnel's
edition of the French New Testament, 1693–4, in 4 vols.,
8vo., including " Moral Reflections on the Gospels, Acts
of the Apostles, and the Epistles," was anathematized
by Pope Clement XI., 1713. His famous bull, Uni-
genitus, is the indelible record of Rome's hostility to the
circulation of the Scriptures.   Forty French Bishops
accepted this bull, which denounced the idea that all
should read the Bible, or that Christians should be
allowed to read it on the Sabbath Day.

Does any one fancy that this warfare with the Bible
ended with the eighteenth century? He should know
of Matamoras, Marin, Carasco, Gonzalez and other
blameless young men, who, but a few years ago,
languished in Spanish prisons until released by the
indignant intercession of the Bible-reading world.
George Borrow was one of the most remarkable English-
men of this generation. Singularly gifted with physical,
mental and personal characteristics for the work, he
spent five years in Spain, endeavoring to circulate the
Scriptures, as he says, " in spite of the opposition and the
furious cry of the sanguinary priesthood and the edicts
of a deceitful government. Throughout my residence
in Spain the clergy were the party from which I
experienced the strongest opposition, and it was at their

instigation that the government originally adopted those measures which prevented any extensive circulation of the volume through the land." Within a few months Spanish secular newspapers have entreated priests and people not to maltreat and mob the Bible colporteur, as the accounts of his sufferings printed in foreign journals are commented upon as though he were exposed to all the dangers of the missionary among savage tribes.

Within our recollection, English travelers have been arrested and imprisoned because single copies of Italian Bibles were found in their portmanteaus when entering the Roman States. Many who read this will remember that before the days of Victor Emmanuel, they found it wise to conceal their copies of Italian Testaments when traveling in Italy, in order to avoid detention and an appeal to the help of their government.

How does the record of the Greek Church compare with that of the Roman, in respect to the Bible? It is better, but at the best it is a record of mere toleration. Neither of these historic churches has ceased to dread the Bible. Its supremacy in the world of printed thought has been attained in the face of a religious hatred deeper and deadlier than that of infidels and atheists.

Literature and printing have furnished no book which remotely resembles the Bible in its career of conflict and triumph; in its universal translation, distribution and domination. Its linguistic influence on the leading languages of civilization is without a parallel. Its authority in morals and religion among enlightened nations has no rival. It is the most powerful ray which penetrates the darkness of this sinful and suffering world.

CHAPTER III.

Manuſcripts.

BOOKS were written, multiplied and circulated during many centuries before the invention of printing. Wiclif translated the Bible into English and multiplied manuscript copies nearly one hundred years before Gutenberg printed his Bible in Latin. Many manuscript copies were made at one time as the transcribers took the words from the lips of a reader. Notwithstanding the Papal war of extermination which followed this effort to give the Bible to the people, a large number of these manuscripts have survived.

Any one familiar with Mediæval writing cannot fail to observe how much the first printed book resembles the best ancient manuscripts. It has been said that this was designed for the purpose of deceiving buyers, who would pay the price of a manuscript for what had been produced by the secret art. There is no proof of this, however, and the resemblance to manuscript is sufficiently accounted for by the fact that the type-maker had no other letters to copy. It cannot be denied that there was great temptation to deceive, for a printed Bible sold at 60 crowns, if equally well done in manuscript, would have cost 500 crowns.

Manuscripts were the employment, enjoyment and glory of the monasteries. Those monks who were specially qualified by learning and skill were appointed to work in the *scriptorium* or *domus antiquariorum*. In Birch and Jenner's work on "Early Drawings and Illuminations in the British Museum," there is an account of their labors. The *antiquarii* prepared copies of old and valuble manuscripts. The *librarii* transcribed more modern works. Here the art of illumination was developed and carried to perfection, in painting miniatures, initials and borders to decorate the pages of written text. Illumination was most richly bestowed on service books for use in the church by ecclesiastics and the more wealthy private worshippers. These books are chiefly Missals, Psalters, and Books of Hours.

The *Missal* is a volume which includes the services relating to the Eucharist, or the celebration of Mass, namely :

1. The *Sacramentary*, containing the Collects, Prefaces, and Canon of the Mass, with occasionally some other Services, such as that of Baptism, etc. 2. The *Lectionary*, containing the Epistles and Gospels, which

are sometimes found in separate books, the Epistle book being then often called the Lectionary. 3. The *Evangeliary, (Evangelarium)*, containing the Gospels arranged for various days; or, the *Evangelia*, containing the four Gospels in their usual order; generally having a portrait of the Evangelist attached to each Gospel. 4. The *Gradual*, containing the Introits, Graduals, (*i. e.*, Psalms and Antiphons preceding the Gospels), Offertories, Communions, *etc.*, set to music. This is still used as a choir book. It is to the *Missal* what the Antiphonary is to the Breviary, and resembles the latter in size and ornament. But in later times the *Missal* became the only book absolutely necessary for the celebration of Mass.

The *Psalter* illuminated was largely used before the fourteenth and fifteenth centuries. When complete *Breviaries* became the rule, these were in a great measure superseded, their contents being included in the Breviaries. The *Breviary* itself is nothing more than the form of recitation of the *Psalter* distributed throughout the one nocturnal and seven daily Services arranged for the seven days of the week, with accompanying lessons, hymns, collects, antiphons, *etc.*, for the most part varying with the season.

The *Book of Hours, Horæ Beatæ Mariæ Virginis*, "Prymer," or by whatever other title it may be known, contains chiefly the "Office of our Lady," from the *Breviary*; with the addition of various prayers and other material. The book was intended for the use of the laity, and was generally adorned with miniatures representing chiefly events in the life of the Virgin Mary. Beautiful specimens of all these sacred and many other manuscript books are to be seen in many of our public and private libraries.

CHAPTER IV.

*

𝕭𝖑𝖔𝖈𝖐 𝕭𝖔𝖔𝖐𝖘.

BLOCK BOOKS, or, *Books of Images*, were the immediate precursors of printing. Their origin and date are doubtful, but they are usually attributed to the early part of the fifteenth century, and to Germany or Holland. They consist of pictorial matter only or mainly. Where they contain any text, it is carved upon the block and thus printed with the pictures. This art of printing from wooden blocks is called Xylography. It is more closely related to the art of wood-engraving than to the art of printing. Both these arts originate in the seals used by the Babylonians in the earliest ages of which we possess historic records. Stamping designs in color from engraved stamps was undoubtedly Roman and Mediæval custom. In the fourteenth century, form-schneiders (model cutters) were abundant in Germany who engraved on wood blocks, patterns to be printed and then colored by hand. It is certain that playing-cards were thus made, and it is probable also that religious pictures and other pictures were produced on this system of pattern-printing and subsequent coloring.

For a long time it was supposed that the oldest extant picture thus made was the St. Christopher of 1423, now in the British Museum. There are, however, numerous pictures, without date, which may be earlier products, and it has never been certain that the date on the St. Christopher was the date of its manufacture. Nor can it be determined whether playing-cards were produced by the form-schneiders' art before religious or other pictures. Much has been written about it, but the subject is in reality of little importance, because the art which produced them was not what we know as either the art of printing or the art of wood-engraving. Printing with movable types was not invented until the middle of the fifteenth century, when Gutenberg produced his Bible at Mentz. Wood-engraving, which produces complete finished pictures printed in ink, was not in use till in the time of Albert Durer toward the end of the fifteenth century. Prior to that time the wood block only impressed a pattern, to be colored by hand, and the picture was complete only when it came from the hand of the painter. All block book pictures and prints prior to Durer's time belong rather to the painter's than the engraver's or printer's art. Durer invented wood-engraving as we know it, the art by which an artist is enabled to reach the public, with his own thoughts, in his own lines, through the printing-press.

Block Books are, nevertheless, among the most precious treasures of bibliography. But few of these xylographic works are known, and of these the most celebrated are the *Biblia Pauperum* and the *Speculum Salvationis*.

The *Biblia Pauperum*, or Bible of the Poor, consists of forty plates, with extracts and sentences analogous to the figures and images represented. The whole is engraven on wood, and printed on one side of the leaves of paper. When folded, the white side of the leaves may be pasted together, so that the number is reduced to twenty. Copies, however, are found, the leaves of which not having been cemented on their blank side, are forty in number, like the plates. Each plate or page contains four busts, two at the top, and two at the bottom, together with three historical subjects; the two upper busts represent the prophets or other persons, whose names are always written beneath them; the two lower busts are anonymous. The middle of the plates, which are all marked by letters of the alphabet in the centre of the upper compartment, is occupied by three historical pictures, one of which is taken from the New Testament. This is the *type* or principal subject, and occupies the centre of the page between two anti-types or other subjects, which relate to it. The inscriptions at the top and bottom of the page consist of texts of Scripture and Leonine verses.

Heinecken, who examined several copies of this work with minute attention, has discovered five different editions of the *Biblia Pauperum ;* the fifth is easily known, as it has *fifty* plates. In executing the other four editions, the engravers, he observes, have worked with such exactness, that there is very little difference between any of them, so that it is impossible to determine which is *the first*.

Though this work is called the "Bible of the Poor," it is not probable that it had any general circulation among the masses. It is more probable that it was used by the poor friars and others who were engaged in religious work.

The *Speculum Humanæ Salvationis*, or Mirror of Salvation, is the most perfect in design and execution of the Books of Images which preceded the invention of printing. It is a small folio, containing sixty-three plates, with accompanying text. There are two Latin editions extant, both of extreme rarity. It was translated into German, Flemish and other languages. The Preface is in rhyming Latin verses printed in long lines. The first two thus announce the title :

Prohemium cujusdam incipit novæ compila=
    tionis ;

Cujus nomen et titulus est speculum humanæ
    salvationis.

The expository matter, at the foot of the different plates, is in two columns. The first plate of the earliest edition is divided into two compartments, separated (as all the other plates are) by a small pillar: that on the left hand exhibits the fall of Lucifer and his angels; in the centre is represented the Saviour, denouncing vengeance against his rebellious subjects, while the angels who retained their allegiance are thrusting them headlong down to hell, whose jaws are widely distended to receive them. Horror and anguish are depicted in the countenances of the fallen spirits who are delineated in the most grotesque attitudes imaginable. Beneath this compartment is inscribed *Casus Luciferi.*

In the right hand compartment is represented the creation of Eve, who is springing out of Adam's side, and is apparently receiving her instructions from the lips of her Creator. The inscription beneath this compartment is, *Dominus creavit homines ad imagines et similitudines suas.* The verses beneath the two columns are illustrative of the general subject of the work. They are as follow:

Incipit Speculum humanæ Saluacionis,
In quo patet casus hominis et modus
    reparacionis.
In hoc speculo potest homo considerare
Quam ob causam creator omnium decrevit
    hominem creare.

**Mulier autem in paradiso est formata,
De costis biri dormientis est parata.**

* * * * * * * * * * * *

These remarks apply to what is reputed to be the first edition, the date of which is not known, but was probably between 1440 and 1457 : the second Latin edition differs from it only in having the whole of the explanatory text printed with fusile types, exactly resembling those emyloyed for part of the letter-press of the first edition. Of the translations into other European languages, the most celebrated is the *Flemish ;* two editions of this are extant, both in folio; and the second differs from the first, chiefly in having the explanatory letter-press of plates 45 and 46 printed with a smaller type.

In the Lenox Library, there is perhaps the finest collection of Block Books in the world. Of the *Biblia Pauperum* there is a copy in a remarkably clean and perfect condition, with the leaves unpasted at the backs and the cuts uncolored; another copy, the first edition in Italian, the only known Italian xylographic work; still another, the second edition in Italian, and two copies in German. There are also copies of other equally rare and celebrated specimens of block books, such as have been bought and sold for several thousand dollars each.

Baron Heinecken published a work on this subject, with the title : "*Idée Générale d'une Collection complette d'Estampes, avec une Dissertation sur l'Origine de la Gravure, et sur les premiers Livres des Images. Leipsic et Vienne,* 1771, 8°." Thomas Hartwell Horne gives an abridgment of this work as far as it relates to *Block Books* or *Books of Images*, in his " Introduction to the Study of Bibliography." It is an interesting fact that the author of that monumental work, " An Introduction to the Critical Study and Knowledge of the Holy Scriptures," which has been an invaluable class-book for thousands of theological students in Great Britain and America, was also the author of two interesting and instructive volumes constituting " An Introduction to the Study of Bibliography, to which is prefixed a Memoir in the Public Libraries of the Antients, 1814, 2 vols., 8vo."

CHAPTER V.

❀

The Gutenberg Bible.

THE FIRST printed book, generally known as The Gutenberg Bible, was produced at Mentz by Gutenberg, some time between 1450 and 1456. It is also known as the *Mazarin Bible*, from the fact that a copy of it was found in the Library of Cardinal Mazarin by William Francis De Bure the younger, who gives an account of the discovery in his "Bibliographie Instructive, tome i., Paris, 1763."

Like many others of the earliest printed books, the Gutenberg Bible has no date, but an inscription by Cremer, the illuminator and binder of the copy in the National Library at Paris, shows that it was printed before 1456.

This splendid production is not only the first printed book, but it is believed to be the first specimen of

printing with movable types extant, with the exception
of certain

Letters of Indulgence.

These letters are the earliest dated specimens of
printing.   Eighteen copies of these are known, all
bearing the printed dates of 1454 or 1455.   Bigmore
and Wyman, in their "Bibliography of Printing," say:
"It is probable that prior to 1450, Gutenberg printed
several small productions, for, had he been uniformly
unsuccessful all these years, he could hardly have been
able to borrow money from time to time.   He possibly
had to leave over, for a more auspicious time, his pro-
jects for printing a large book, and to content himself
with 'jobbing-work,' as it would now be called."

Dr. Dibdin, in his "Bibliotheca Spenceriana," gives
a transcript of one of these Letters of Indulgence, in
connection with historic details, referring to the labors
of Lambinet and Haeberlin.   He says: "In the year
1452 the Turks carried fire and sword into Epirus, and
almost the whole of Greece.   Cyprus was menaced; the
Pontiff wrote to John II. to fortify the walls of his
capital, Nicosia, and to resist the attacks of the Mussul-
man: promising to defray the expenses attending this
measure, by the sums of money which his Letters of
Indulgence might produce.   This epistle is dated in
June, 1452.   Pope Nicolas V., died at Rome in March,
1455."   To one of the copies of these earliest surviving
specimens of printing, is still appended the original
Papal seal.

As no other book equals in bibliographical interest,

𝕿𝖍𝖊 𝕲𝖚𝖙𝖊𝖓𝖇𝖊𝖗𝖌 𝕭𝖎𝖇𝖑𝖊,

we give the following description at length.   The first
volume begins as follows :

> 𝕴𝖓𝖈𝖎𝖕𝖎𝖙 𝖊𝖕𝖎𝖘𝖙𝖔𝖑𝖆 𝖘𝖆𝖓𝖈𝖙𝖎 𝖎𝖍𝖊𝖗𝖔𝖓𝖎𝖒𝖎 𝖆𝖉
> 𝖕𝖆𝖚𝖑𝖎𝖓𝖚𝖒 𝖕𝖗𝖊𝖘𝖇𝖎𝖙𝖊𝖗𝖚𝖒 𝖉𝖊 𝖔𝖒𝖓𝖎𝖇𝖚𝖘
> 𝖉𝖎𝖚𝖎𝖓𝖊 𝖍𝖎𝖘𝖙𝖔𝖗𝖎𝖊 𝖑𝖎𝖇𝖗𝖎𝖘. 𝖈𝖆𝖕𝖎𝖙𝖚𝖑𝖚̄ 𝖕̄𝖒𝖚̄.

> [F] **R**ater ambrosius
> tua michi manus=
> cula pferens. detulit
> fil⁹ et suauissimas
> lrās: q̃ a principio
> amiciciaꝫ fide. pba=
> te iam fidei: ꝛ veteris amicicie noua

The *first* volume has 324 leaves, the *second* 317
leaves, being 641 to the whole work.   In the first nine
pages there are 40 lines in a column ; in the tenth, 41 ;
and in the remainder, 42 lines.   The columns, two in
number on each page, are $11\frac{1}{4}$ inches in height ; $3\frac{3}{4}$ in
breadth ; and there is a space of seven-eighths of an
inch between them.   The type is a large Gothic or
German character.   The letter *(i)* is printed in various
ways : sometimes it has a dot *(i)*, at others a dash *(i)*,
and frequently a circumflex *(î)*.   Masch (*Bibliotheca
Sacra*, vol. iii., *p.* 67) considers the latter to have been
used when the *i* was to be pronounced long ; but this is
not borne out by the instances which every page can

afford. De Bure regards it as the effect of an imperfection
in the art of printing. There are neither signatures,
catchwords, numerals, nor running titles. The paper is
of very firm and good texture, and the water-marks are
a Bull's Head, with a Star and a Bunch of Grapes.

The FIRST VOLUME contains the Prologues of St.
Jerome, (8 pages), the Pentateuch, and the other books
of the Old Testament as far as the Psalms. The SECOND
VOLUME begins with the Prologue of St. Jerome on the
books of Solomon, and contains the remaining books
of the Old Testament, and the whole of the New
Testament.

There are two copies in the National Library at Paris,
one upon vellum, bound in four volumes, and the other
upon paper, in two volumes. The latter copy has a
subscription in red ink at the end of each volume. That
at the end of the *first* volume, of which a fac-simile is
given in the *Classical Journal*, vol. IV., *p.* 481, is as
follows :

> Et sic est finis prime partis biblie
> seu veteris testamenti. Illuminata
> seu rubricata et ligata p̄ henricum
> Albch̄ alius Cremer Anno d̄m̄ mcccc
> lvi festo Bartholomei apli
> Deo gracias . . . . . . Alleluia.

TRANSLATION.

*"Here ends the first part of the Bible or Old Testament.
Illuminated, or rubricated, and bound, by Henry Albch or Cremer,
on St. Bartholomew's day, April, A. D. 1456. Thanks be to
God. Hallelujah."*

At the end of the second volume the subscription is:

𝔈𝔰𝔱𝔢 𝔩𝔦𝔟𝔢𝔯 𝔦𝔩𝔩𝔲𝔪𝔦𝔫𝔞𝔱𝔲𝔰 𝔩𝔦𝔤𝔞𝔱𝔲𝔰 𝔢𝔱 𝔠𝔬𝔪𝔭𝔩𝔢𝔠𝔱𝔲𝔰 𝔢𝔰𝔱 𝔭 𝔥𝔢𝔫𝔯𝔦𝔠𝔲𝔪 𝔈𝔯𝔢𝔪𝔢𝔯, 𝔟𝔦𝔠𝔞𝔯𝔦𝔲 𝔢𝔠𝔠𝔩𝔢𝔰𝔢 𝔠𝔬𝔩𝔩𝔢= 𝔤𝔦𝔞𝔱𝔢 𝔰𝔞𝔫𝔠𝔱𝔦 𝔖𝔱𝔢𝔭𝔥𝔞𝔫𝔦 𝔪𝔞𝔤𝔲𝔫𝔱𝔦𝔫𝔦 𝔰𝔲𝔟 𝔞𝔫𝔫𝔬 𝔡𝔫𝔦 𝔪𝔦𝔩𝔩𝔢𝔰𝔦𝔪𝔬 𝔮𝔲𝔞𝔱𝔯𝔦𝔫𝔤𝔢𝔫𝔱𝔢𝔰𝔦𝔪𝔬 𝔮𝔲𝔦𝔫𝔮𝔲𝔞𝔤𝔢𝔰𝔦𝔪𝔬 𝔰𝔢𝔵𝔱𝔬, 𝔰𝔢𝔰𝔱𝔬 𝔞𝔰𝔰𝔲𝔪𝔭𝔱𝔦𝔬𝔫𝔦𝔰 𝔤𝔩𝔬𝔯𝔦𝔬𝔰𝔢 𝔳𝔦𝔯𝔤𝔦𝔫𝔦𝔰 𝔐𝔞𝔯𝔦𝔢. 𝔇𝔢𝔬 𝔊𝔯𝔞𝔠𝔦𝔞𝔰. 𝔄𝔩𝔩𝔢𝔩𝔲𝔦𝔞.

TRANSLATION.

"*This book, illuminated and bound by Henry Cremer, vicar of the collegiate church of St. Stephen, at Mentz, was completed on the feast of the assumption of the Blessed Virgin Mary, A. D. 1456. Thanks be to God. Hallelujah.*"

In order to produce this great folio Bible Gutenberg had exhausted his resources, and borrowed from relatives and friends. John Fust, or Faust, twice lent him 800 guilders, taking a mortgage on all his printing materials. Gutenberg's splendid achievement in the new art was not a financial success. In order to recover his money Fust brought a suit against the inventor, which resulted in the removal of all his printing materials to the house of Fust, and Gutenberg went forth penniless. He was assisted by Dr. Humery in establishing another press in the same neighborhood, but he did not prosper. In 1465 he became a pensioner at the court of Archbishop Adolphus, and died soon after in 1468.

His invention has always been a marvel in respect to the perfection of its beginning. No one looks at the earliest specimens of printing without being astonished at their clearness and beauty. " It is a very striking circumstance," says Hallam," " that the high-minded inventors of this great art tried, at the very outset, so bold a flight as the printing of an entire Bible, and executed it with astonishing success. It was Minerva leaping on earth in her divine strength and radiant armor, ready at the moment of her nativity to subdue and destroy her enemies. We may see in imagination this venerable and splendid volume leading up the crowded myriads of its followers, and imploring, as it were, a blessing on the new art, by dedicating its first fruits to the service of Heaven."

Just what Gutenberg accomplished in perfecting the art of printing, is made plain by Mr. De Vinne in his " Invention of Printing," when he says that Gutenberg's *brass mould for making types* was the key to the invention :

" Gutenberg, first of all, made types in brass moulds and matrices. In other words, it was only through the invention of matrices and type-mould in brass that printing became a great art. Considered from a mechanical point of view, the merit of Gutenberg's invention may be inferred from its permanency. His type-mould was not merely the first, it is the only practical mechanism in making types. For more than four hundred years this mould has been under critical examination, and many attempts have been made to supplant it. Contrivances have been invented for casting fifty or more types at one operation; for swaging types, like nails, out of cold metal; for stamping types from cylindrical steel dyes upon the ends of thin copper rods, but experience has shown that these and like inventions in the department of type-making machinery are impracticable. There is no better method than Gutenberg's. Modern type-casting machines have moulds attached to them which are more exact and more carefully finished, and which have many little attachments of which Gutenberg never dreamed, but in principle and in all the more important features, the modern moulds may be regarded as the moulds of Gutenberg." Every one who reads should know this, at least, of the first printer and the first printed book.

Besides the Letters of Indulgence, the Bible, a few pamphlets and small quartos of a few leaves each, Gutenberg printed a splendid volume — a folio of 748 pages — *The Catholicon.* It was written or edited by John, of Genoa, a mendicant friar, and contains a Latin Grammar and Dictionary. The colophon states that it was printed at Mentz in 1460, but does not give the name of the printer. A copy of the *Catholicon* is to be seen in the Lenox Library, and also in the Astor Library. Another remarkably fine copy is in the library of Mr. Brayton Ives, New York City. The copy from the Syston Park Library, recently sold in London for $2,000, is in the Brown Library, at Providence, R. I.

Mr. De Vinne says: "The silence of Gutenberg concerning his services is remarkable, all the more so when this silence is contrasted with the silly chatterings of several printers during the last quarter of the fifteenth century — of whom Peter Schoeffer may be considered as the first, and Trechsel of Lyons the last — each insisting that he, whatever others might have done before him, was the true perfecter of printing. There is no other instance in modern history, excepting possibly that of Shakespeare, of a man who did so much and who said so little about it."

There is evidence that Gutenberg died before February, 1468. It was believed that he was buried in the Church of St. Frances, at Mentz. This church, which contained his tomb, was destroyed in 1742. Ivo Wittig, Chancellor and Rector of the University of Mayence, placed a tablet in the court of the house of the Gensfleisch family at Mayence, with the inscription: "To John Gutenberg, of Mayence, who first of all invented printing-letters in brass, [matrices and moulds], by which art he has deserved honour from the whole world."

In 1837, Thorwaldsen's monument to Gutenberg was erected at Mayence, in one of the public squares, called Gutenberg Platz. Gutenberg is represented as standing with one foot slightly advanced, holding his BIBLE clasped to his breast with one hand, while several punches are lightly grasped in the other. In a series of bas-reliefs upon the pedestal are seen the processes of the art in its earliest stages. The inscription states that the monument was erected by the citizens of Mayence, with the assistance of the whole of Europe.

In 1840, a statue of Gutenberg, by the celebrated French sculptor, David d'Angers, was erected in the market-place of Strasburg, called La Place Gutenberg. The figure stands erect holding forth a sheet with the words from Genesis, "Et la lumière fut." Upon the pedestal four bas-reliefs illustrate the dissemination of knowledge by means of the printing-press, and on the front various great authors of Europe are grouped around a printing-press. A copy of the David monument stands in the great court of the Imprimerie Nationale at Paris.

There is a monument to Gutenberg in the city of Frankfort. Upon a lofty pedestal of fine, red sandstone stand three colossal figures in electro-plated copper, the central figure being Gutenberg, with a type in his hand, while Schœffer stands on his right and Fust on his left. Four sitting figures on the corners of the pedestal represent Theology, Poetry, Natural Science, and Industry. Upon the upper part of the pedestal, medallions contain the heads of celebrated printers. "But why," says Madden, "should we speak of monuments of bronze or stone to commemorate the services of Gutenberg? His monument is in every quarter of the world: more frail than all, it is more enduring than all — it is the BOOK!"

𝕰𝖝𝖙𝖆𝖓𝖙 𝕮𝖔𝖕𝖎𝖊𝖘.

The following list of known copies of the Gutenberg
Bible was compiled by Dr. S. Austin Allibone of the
Lenox Library, New York, in 1882:

COPIES ON VELLUM.

1. National Library, Paris.

2. Royal Library, Berlin.

3. British Museum.

4. Earl of Ashburton's Library.

5. Leipsic Library.

6. Heinrich Klemm, Dresden.

7. Library at Dresden: a fragment only.

COPIES ON PAPER.

1. National Library, Paris.

2. Mazarin Library, Paris.

3. Imperial Library, Vienna.

4. Public Library, Treves.

5. Bodleian Library, Oxford.

6. Advocates' Library, Edinburgh.

7. Geo. III$^{d's}$ Library, British Museum.

8. Duke of Sussex's Library.

9. Duke of Devonshire's Library.

10. Earl Spencer's Library.

11. Lenox Library, New York.

12. Library of John Fuller.

13. Lloyd's Library.

14. Leipsic Library.

15. Munich Library.

16. Frankfort Library.

17. Hanover Library.

18. Emperor of Russia's Library.

19. Library at Mentz.

20. Huth Library.

21. Library of Hamilton Cole, New York, (now in the Library of Brayton Ives, New York).

To this list must be added the Syston Park copy recently sold, and the Earl of Crawford's copy, sold still more recently, unless both of these copies are in the list under names that have changed with ownership during recent years. It is worthy of note that there is no record of a copy being in the Vatican Library at Rome. These copies are not all alike in size, or in the style of their illumination, or in the number of lines on all pages. It appears that there were two issues, one with 42 lines on all the pages, the other with 40 lines on the first eight pages, 41 lines on the ninth page, and the rest with 42 lines. Other variations in the number of lines are mentioned by different bibliographers.

The LENOX COPY is on paper, in two volumes. It was formerly in the Library of George Hibbert, Esq., which was sold at auction in London in 1829. It was bought by Mr. Wilkes for £215, about $1,075. It was sold again in 1848, and bought by Mr. Lenox for about $2,500. This copy is now worth as many thousand dollars as it then cost hundreds.

Until recently, the highest price ever paid for a printed book was at the Henry Perkins Library Sale in London, 1873, when a vellum copy of the Gutenberg Bible sold for £3,400, or about $16,500. A paper copy brought at the same sale, £2,690. These figures have since been surpassed at the Syston Park Library Sale in London, when a paper copy was sold to Mr. Quaritch, the bookseller, for £3,900, or nearly $20,000.

Unless the descriptions of this copy by foreign correspondents are grossly incorrect, the Lenox copy is much finer, and therefore much more valuable than the one recently sold for nearly $20,000.

But the highest price known to have been paid for a printed book was given at this Syston Park Sale for the book which is the subject of the next chapter.

The only other copy of the Gutenberg Bible in America is The BRAYTON IVES COPY. In size and condition it is a splendid specimen, not having suffered, as other famous copies, at the hands of the binders. Its ancient binding still remains to show the wisdom, taste and skill with which it was first protected and adorned. Seventeen leaves scattered through the two volumes are in *fac-simile*, but in other respects this copy is superior to copies which have escaped this necessity. It is the 42 line issue, which is considered the first. With its unimpaired margins, beautiful print, perfect register, cleanly condition, interesting binding and other features, it ranks very high among the few specimens remaining of the first printed book and the first printed Bible.

Mr. Theodore Irwin, of Oswego, N. Y., has a volume of the Gutenberg Bible, containing the Old Testament and Apocrypha to the end of the Books of Maccabees. It is one of the 42 line copies, and has 513 leaves, with only one leaf and a portion of another in *facsimile*. When bought, this copy was in the original pigskin binding, in oak boards.

CHAPTER VI.

✳

The Mentz Psalter. 1457.

THE FIRST BOOK WITH DATE—THE SECOND PRINTED BOOK.

THE MENTZ PSALTER, or, *Psalmorum Codex*, being an edition of the Psalms in Latin, is the first book known which contains the name of its printer together with the name of the place where it was printed, and the date of its execution. It is a folio of 175 leaves, with initial letters in two colors. It was printed by *Fust* and *Schoffer* at Mentz, and was finished August 14th, 1457, during the brief period between the first and second printed Bibles. Its extreme rarity has given it extraordinary pecuniary value, a very few copies being known. Until recently, the highest price ever paid for a printed book was given for a copy of the Gutenberg Bible, $16,500, at the Perkins Sale, London, 1873. This was surpassed at the Syston Park Sale, London, December, 1884, when a paper copy of the Gutenberg

Bible was sold for £3,900, and a vellum copy of the Mentz Psalter was sold for £4,950, nearly $25,000.

After Gutenberg had printed the first Bible, his creditor, Fust, obtained possession of all his printing materials.   Fust formed a partnership with Peter Schoffer, who became his son-in-law.   Their first publication was the Mentz Psalter, the first printed book with a complete date.   This was reprinted with the same types in 1459, 1490, 1502 and 1516.   The copy recently sold for nearly $25,000 is the second edition. It is entered in the Sale Catalogue of the Syston Park Library as follows:

"*Psalmorum Codex, Latine cum Hymnis, Oratione Dominica Symbolis ei Notis musicis.*   Printed on Vellum, very fine copy, with painted capitals, in red morocco extra, borders of gold, gilt edges, by Staggemeier, folio. Moguntiæ, J. Fust et P. Schoffer, 1459.

" This excessively rare edition is the second book with a date, and contains the Athanasian Creed, printed for the first time.   In rarity it nearly equals that printed in 1457, of which only eight copies are known, and of this only ten, all printed on vellum.   This copy sold for 3,350 francs in the MacCarthy Sale, and £136 10 s. in that of Sir M. Sykes."

A copy of this edition is in the British Museum, and also a copy of the first edition, printed on vellum, which is not only the first book printed with a date, but the first example of printing in colors.

Beautiful *fac-similes* of pages of this Psalter are in

Dibdin's " Bibliotheca Spenceriana," and in Humphrey's " History of Printing," and also in the more accessible volume, Theodore L. De Vinne's " Invention of Printing."

In the Caxton Exhibition, London, 1877, the 1457 copy of this Psalter was lent by the Queen, and the 1459 copy by the Earl of Leicester. No copy of this book is in America.

The most perfect copy known is in the Imperial Library of Vienna. It was discovered in the year 1665, near Innspruck, in the castle of Ambras, where the arch-duke, Francis Sigismund, had collected an immense number of manuscripts and printed books, taken for the most part from the famous library of Matthias Corvinus, King of Hungary. It is a folio of 175 leaves, printed on vellum, of which the Psalter occupies the first 135 and the *recto* of the 136th. The remainder is appropriated to the litany, prayers, responses, vigils, etc. The psalms are executed in larger characters than the hymns, similar to those used for missals prior to the invention of printing, but all are distinguished for their uncommon blackness. The capital letters, 288 in number, are cut on wood, with a degree of delicacy and boldness which are sur-prising. The largest of these, the initial letters of the Psalms, which are black, red and blue, must have passed *three* times through the press. A *fac-simile* of the first initial letter of this splendid Psalter is given with a few sentences of the first psalm, in Dibdin's *Bibliotheca Spenceriana*, vol. i., p. 107, colored exactly after the

original.   As it is scarcely possible that this masterpiece
of the typographical art could be executed within
eighteen months after the dissolution of partnership
between Gutenberg and Fust, Fournier and Meerman
conjecture that it was begun during its continuance,
though finished by Fust and Schoffer.

This Mentz Psalter, being second only to the Gutenberg
Bible in bibliographical interest, we give the following
description :

The work begins on the recto of the first leaf, with
two musical-scored lines at top.   The lines and the
notes are inserted in manuscript as well as the words
"Venite exulte," etc.   The text begins about three
inches below.   A full page, which is 7 inches and $\frac{5}{8}$ in
breadth, by about $11\frac{1}{4}$ in height, contains 20 lines.   It
is not printed in type of uniform size.   The collects,
responses, verses and prayers, are generally in a smaller
type.   The colophon, which is also printed in the small
type, and with red ink, is literally as follows :

**Pſis ſpalmoʒ coder. benuſtate capitaliū decoātꝰ
Rubricationibuſcꝫ ſuſſcienter diſtinctus,
Adinuētione artiſicōſa impmendi ac caracteriʒ=
andi. abſcꝫ calami blla eraracōne ſic eſſgiatus,
Et ad euſebiam dei induſtrie eſt ꝛſummatus,
Per Joh'em Fuſt Ciuē magūtinū. Et Petrū
Schoffer de Gernſʒheim, Anno dñi Milleſiō.
cccc. lbij. In bigl'ia Aſſūpcōis.**

TRANSLATION.

"*This work of the Psalms, a book embellished with beautiful capitals, and sufficiently distinguished with rubric letters, was thus formed by an ingenious invention of printing, with separate characters, without any writing of the pen, and carefully finished for the worship of God, by* JOHN FUST, *Citizen of Mentz, and* PETER SCHOFFER, *of Gernszheim ; in the year of the Lord one thousand four hundred and fifty-seven. On the eve of the Assumption (August 14.)*"

The second edition of this Psalter, printed in 1459, a folio, by the same printers, varies in many respects from the preceding. Though executed with the same types and capital letters, the lines are longer in this second edition, with **23** on a page, whereas the *first* edition has but **20** lines on a page. According to Heinecken, who is followed by Lichtenberger and others, a complete copy contains 163 leaves; but Wurdtwein, who appears to have examined it with more minuteness, states it to consist of only 136. Dibdin conjectures the difference to have been caused by the figures being transposed by Heinecken's printer.

The text begins at the top of the page with the following words:

Beatus vir qui nō abijt in cōſilio impioʒ.

The colophon, which we transcribe *verbatim et literatim*, is on the reverse of fol. 151, and is printed in red ink :

𝕻Refens pfalmoꝛ coder : benuftate capitaliū. decoratus. rubricationibufꝗ fufficienter diftinctus. ad inuencōne artifficiofa imprimendi ac caracterizandi : abfꝗ ulla calami eraracōne fic efffgiatus. et ad laudem dei ac honorē fancti Jacobi eft ꝛfūatꝰ. Per Joh'em Fuft cibē magū= tinū. et Petrū Schoiffer de Gernffheim clericū Anno dūi Millefimo cccc. lir. rrir die menfis Augufti.   [Mentz.] 1459. *fol.*

CHAPTER VII.

✻

The Bamberg Bible. (1460?)

THE SECOND PRINTED BIBLE.

THE SECOND BIBLE is generally known as *The Bamberg Bible*, from the place where it is believed to have been printed; or the *Pfister Bible*, from the name of its supposed printer; or the *Bible of Thirty-six Lines*, from the number of lines on a page. Like other printed books of this period, it has no title-page or date. In the Catalogue of the Caxton Exhibition the copy of this Bible, lent by Earl Spencer, is entered as follows:

"Bible (Second Latin). Gothic Letter. (Bamberg: Albert Pfister, 1460?). Folio: 15¾ by 11 inches. Without title, pagination or signatures. 882 leaves; printed in double columns, 36 lines to a full column. A copy in the Paris Library has the rubrication dated 1461, proving that this Bible was printed prior to that date.

But the cover of the Church Register of Bamberg being composed partly of waste leaves of this Bible, and the Register beginning with 21 March, 1460, it follows that these leaves were printed prior to this latter date."

Albert Pfister is believed to have been a workman of Gutenberg, who established a press at Bamberg, near which city nearly all the copies of this Bible were found.

Mr. De Vinne, in his work on the "Invention of Printing," gives at length the reasons for the opinion that this Bible is not the work of Pfister, but one of the earlier works of Gutenberg, and therefore not the second Bible, but the first. He says: "In nearly all the popular treatises on printing the *Bible of Forty-two Lines* is specified as the first book of Gutenberg, but it is the belief of many of the most learned bibliographers, from Zapf to Didot and Madden, that the Bible of thirty-six lines is the older edition." Mr. Hawkins favors this view, saying: "It seems to me that this Bible must have been produced by the same set of workmen who printed the Gutenberg Bible; many points of resemblance in each edition lead to this conclusion. I am not of those who believe that the Gutenberg Bible was the result of a first experiment. Years of patient labor must have been spent and many vexatious failures and partial successes experienced before this splendid work was produced. Might not the Bible of thirty-six lines have been produced by Gutenberg during these years of experiment? I do not assert this, but merely suggest its probability.

At all events, I venture the assertion that there is no convincing evidence that it was printed by Pfister at Bamberg or elsewhere."

Notwithstanding these well-considered views of American students of early printing, we are compelled to record this Bible of thirty-six lines as the second, as there is as yet no evidence that it was printed before 1455, the latest date assigned to the Gutenberg Bible. Of Pfister nothing is known but his name and a few books and pamphlets attributed to him. His earliest dated book is the *Book of Fables*, 1461. Mr. De Vinne says that the profusion of wood-cuts in this and his other books indicates that he was an engraver on wood. He thinks that he bought an old font of type to use in printing the explanations of these pictures. His *Book of Four Stories*, with his imprint, Bamberg, 1462, is printed with the types of the *Bible of Thirty-six Lines*, and this gave the impression that he printed this Bible also. Sebastian Pfister, supposed to be his son, had a printing office at Bamberg in 1470. Although next to nothing is known of Albert Pfister, his name has been used as a rival to that of Gutenberg for the honor of the invention of the art of printing.

We give the following descriptive points which are sufficient to enable any one to identify a copy of this one of the earliest printed books :

Biblia Sacra Latina. [Bamberg: Albert Pfister, 1460?] *Gothic letter*, 3 vols., folio.

The work commences on the recto of the first leaf, at the top of the first column, which begins five lines below the top of the second, thus —

> [F] **Rater am=**
> **brosius mi=**
> **chi tua munuscula perferens de=**
> **tulit simul. et suauissimas litte=**
> **ras: que a principio amiticiaꝛ**
> **fidem iam p̄bate fidei et veteris**
> **amicicie noua preferebant. Ue=**
> * * * * * * * * * * *

The first chapter of Genesis begins at the top of the first column, on the reverse of fol. VI., as follows :—

> [IN] **principio creauit deus celū ꝛ**
> **terram. Terra āut erat inanis**
> **et uacu: et tenebre erāt sup fa=**
> **ciem abissi: et spirit⁹ dn̄i fereba=**
> **tur aꝗas.**

The first volume ends at the bottom of the first column of the last leaf, thus —

> **rege per singulos dies omnib⁹**
> **diebus uite sue.**

The second volume begins with St. Jerome's Prologue to the Books of Chronicles; and ends with Maccabees at the bottom of the last column, on the recto of the last leaf.

The third volume begins with St. Jerome's Letter to Pope Damasus concerning the Four Gospels. The first five lines are indented, to make room for the letter B. It ends on the reverse of the last leaf, at top of the second column, with :

> 𝕯icit, q̃ teſti=
> monium perhibet iſtorum Eti=
> am. Uenio cito amen. Ueni do=
> mine iheſu. 𝕲racia domini no=
> ſtri iheſu criſti cum omnibȝ uo=
> bis amen.

Without pagination or signatures; printed in double columns, 36 lines to a full column. According to Hain, and Masch, a perfect copy contains 264 leaves in the first volume, 310 in the second, and 296 in the third: 870 leaves in the whole work.

CHAPTER VIII.

The Mentelin Bible. (1460-1461?)

THE THIRD PRINTED BIBLE.

THE THIRD BIBLE is generally known as *The Mentelin Bible* from the name of its printer, Johannes Mentelin, or, *The Strasburg Bible*, from the name of the place where it was printed.

It is thus entered in the Catalogue of the Caxton Exhibition:

Biblia Sacra Latina. (Third Latin Bible.) Strasburg: Jo. Mentelin, 1460 and 1461? 2 vols., folio. $15\frac{3}{4}$ by $11\frac{3}{4}$ inches. *Lent by Earl Spencer.* Without title-page, pagination, or signatures; 477 leaves, printed in double columns, 49 lines to a full column. The rubrics and initials are in MS. throughout. A copy of this Bible is preserved in the library of Freiburg in Breisgau, with the rubrications of the volumes dated 1460 and 1461, ranking this edition as the third Latin Bible."

There is a copy of this Bible on exhibition in the Lenox Library.

Mr. Hawkins gives this Bible the second place, and says: "A copy of this Bible in the University Library at Freiburg, in Breisgau, Baden, is in two volumes; has at the end of the first this inscription: 'Explicit psalteriũ 1460;' and at the end of the second, 'Explicit Apocalipsis Anno dñi MoCCCCLXI.' The authenticity of the inscriptions is vouched for by the fact that they were made by the same hand which rubricated every page in both volumes. Accepting these dates as made in good faith, a press must have been set up at Strasburg as early as 1459, which would entitle that city to the position, in the history of printing, which has usually been assigned to Bamberg, since the first volume of the Mentelin edition has an implied earlier date than any known copy of the so-called Bamberg Bible. I am therefore compelled to give Strasburg the second place in the chronological arrangement which I have adopted."

Lack of positive information makes abundant room for difference of opinion and arrangement. Such historical puzzles are an agreeable form of intellectual recreation. They also keep inquiring minds from those prophetic problems which lead so many uninspired men into manifest absurdities. The future never fails to make itself known in good season, but we must look after the past, or it will escape us entirely.

It is now considered probable that Strasburg received

the art of printing from Mentz, at least as early as
Bamberg. Mentelin is believed to have printed *the first
Bible in German*, the Epistles of St. Jerome, and several
other large folios. He was buried in the Strasburg
Cathedral, which contains a tablet with a magniloquent
inscription, attributing to him the invention and develop-
ment of the art of printing. This claim, like that of
many others, was not made until long after his death,
and is not supported by public or private records. He
was for a time in partnership with Henry Eggesteyn,
became prosperous as a publisher, issued descriptive
catalogues, and employed agents for the sale of his
works. Philip de Lignamine, of Rome, in 1474, said
that Mentelin printed in Strasburg after 1458.

We give the following descriptive points of The
Third Bible:

Biblia Sacra Latina. [Strasburg: Jo. Mentelin,
1460 and 1461?] 2 vols., folio.

(F. 1 a :) **Rater ambrosius tua/michi munus=
cula perfe/res. detulit fi⁹ et suauissimas lras. q̄
a principio/ amiciciaru. fide probate**/*etc.*

(F. 3 b., col. 1, l. 36 :) [N] **principio creauit deus
celu et tram./Terra autem erat inanis et vacua :
et tenebre/erant sup facie abissi. & spus dni fer=
ebat super**/*etc.*

(F. 215 a, col. 2, l. 46, explicit. Psalt. :) **omnis spir=
itus laudet dominum. Alleluia.**

(F. 216 a :) [ ] **ungat epistola quos iugit facer=**

dotíum: ímmo / carta non díuídat: quos ȑpí
nectít amor. con/*etc.*

(F. 342a, col. 1, l. 38, term. V. T.:)   non erít
gratus: híc ergo erít confummatus.

(Seq. Ep. S. Hieronymi:)   [ ] eatíffímo pape
damafo íero=/nímus. Nouum opus me/facere
cogís er beterí: ut poft/eremplaría fcrípturarū
toto/*etc.*

(N. T. expl. fol. 427a, col. 1, l. 42:)   Gratía dñí
nȓí íh9u ȑpí cū omíb9 bobís amen.

GOTHIC LETTER. Without date, place of imprint, and
name of printer; 477 leaves, printed in double columns,
49 lines to a full column, and without pagination, or
signatures.

CHAPTER IX.

❀

Ͳ𝔥𝔢 𝔉𝔦𝔯𝔰𝔱 𝔇𝔞𝔱𝔢𝔡 𝔅𝔦𝔟𝔩𝔢. (1462).

THE FOURTH PRINTED BIBLE.

THE FOURTH BIBLE is unique in this respect, that it is *the first edition of the Bible with the date, name* of printer, and *place* where printed. It was printed by Fust and Schoffer, at Mentz, 1462. 2 vols. Gothic letter. Three copies of this were in the Caxton Exhibition, one on pure vellum richly illuminated in gold and colors, lent by Earl Spencer, another equally rich lent by Earl Jersey, and a third copy, on paper, lent by Mr. Stevens. At the Syston Park Sale, a copy of this Bible on vellum sold for $5,000.

This fourth Bible brings us back to the city where the art of printing originated. Gutenberg's first book and Bible, though cherished to this day as one of the most splendid specimens of typography, was a financial disaster. As the result of a law suit, his office and materials passed into the hands of his creditor, Fust, who formed a partnership with Peter Schoffer, and these two became Gutenberg's successors in Mentz. Their Bible, the first with a date and name of printer, and place where printed, is usually called *the Bible of 1462.* Both the Lenox and Astor Libraries have a copy of this Bible on exhibition. This Fust, who is so closely associated with Gutenberg, has been confused in literature and legend with Dr. John Faust, a somewhat mythical character, who was born after the death of Gutenberg, and whose career as a magician is the foundation of many tales in prose and poetry. Historical students do not give any credit to the old, old story, thus told by D'Israeli, relating to this very Bible of 1462 :

" A considerable number of copies of the Bible were printed to imitate Manuscripts, and the sale of them in Paris entrusted to Fust, as MSS. Consequent upon his selling them at sixty crowns per copy, whilst the other scribes demanded five hundred, universal astonishment was created, and still more when he produced copies as fast as they were wanted, and even lowered the price. The uniformity of the copies increased the wonder. Informations were given in to the magistrates against him as a magician, and on searching his lodgings a great number of copies were found. The red ink (and Fust's red ink is peculiarly brilliant) which embellished his copies was said to be his blood, and it was solemnly adjudged that he was in league with the infernals. Fust at length was obliged (to save himself from a bonfire) to reveal his art to the parliament of Paris, who discharged him from all prosecution in consideration of the wonderful invention."

Mr. De Vinne sums up the facts of the case in the following paragraph : " Eager to prevent the threatened rivalry of Jenson, Fust appeared in Paris, in 1462, with copies of the Bible, while Jenson was ineffectually soliciting the new King to aid him. So far from being persecuted in Paris, Fust was received with high consideration, not only by the King, but by the leading men of the city. He was encouraged to establish in Paris a store for the sale of his books and to repeat his visit." He is believed to have died of the plague in Paris in 1466, where he was buried in the Church of Saint Victor.

Besides his famous Bible of 1462 and the equally famous *Mentz Psalters*, 1457–59, etc., Fust published the *Rationale Divinorum Officiorum*, 1459, an exposition of the services of the church by Durandus. This is the third book with a date. Copies of this book can be seen at both the Astor and Lenox Libraries. Besides other large theological works, Fust and Schoffer printed *the first edition of a classic, Cicero de Officiis*, 1465, a small quarto of eighty-eight leaves. It contains the following colophon: "This very celebrated work of Marcus Tullius, I, John Fust, a citizen of Mentz, have happily completed through the hands of Peter, my son, not with writing ink, nor with pen, nor yet in brass, but with a certain art exceedingly beautiful. Dated 1465." It is pleasant to know that the first secular writing of

any importance to be committed to the press was one
of the purest and noblest of the productions of antiquity,
a work akin to the Bible in being a treatise on moral
obligations, and by its very excellence revealing the
infinite distance between the Word of God and the best
utterances of an uninspired mind.   It is fitting that the
first and grandest of the earliest printed books should
be the Bible.   It is also fitting that the first classic
author to appear in this marvelous form should be one
who was an enthusiastic lover and collector of literary
treasures.   A copy of this book is to be seen at the
Astor Library.

We give a few descriptive points that identify the
Fourth Printed Bible :

VOLUME FIRST ends with the Psalms, and contains
242 leaves.   The Epistle of St. Jerome begins at the top
of the first column, on the recto of the first leaf, the first
two lines, forming the prefix, are printed in red.

Jncip epl⁹a ſcī iheronimi aꝺ paulinū ꝓſbite=
rū: ꝺe om̄ibꜩ ꝺiuine hiſtorie libris. ca. ꝓmū.

[F] Rater ambroſius tua
michi munuſcula pfe=
rens. ꝺetulit ſimul et
ſuauiſſimas lᷓas: q̄ a
pīncipio. amiciciaꝝ fi=
ꝺem. pbate iam fiꝺei:
et veteris amicicie no=
ua ꝓferebant. vera enī illa neceſſituꝺo ꞇ.

At the bottom of the second column on the verso of the last leaf is the date, and device of the printers, printed in red:

Anno 𝔐. **.cccc.lxij.**

Volume Second, contains 239 leaves, and begins with the following summary printed in red:

Epiſtola ſancti ieronimi preſbiteri ad chro matiū et eliodorū epos de libris ſalomonis.

The volume concludes with the Apocalypse: "Explicit liber apocalipsis beati iohannis apl'l," printed in red, and the following colophon, also in red:

Pñs hoc opuſculū Artificioſa adinuētione impmendi ſeu caracterizandi abſq̃ calami exaracōn. in ciuitate 𝔐oguntū ſic effigiatu. ꝫ ad euſebiā dei induſtrie per Joh'ez Fuſt ciue Petrū ſchoiſfher de gernſ'heym, clericū di= oteſ⁹ eiuſdem eſt conſūmatuꝫ. Anno dñi 𝔐. cccc. lxij. In vigilia aſſumpcōis virḡ. marie.

CHAPTER X.

✱

𝕷𝖆𝖙𝖎𝖓 𝕭𝖎𝖇𝖑𝖊𝖘.

IN 1462, during a war between two archbishops, Mentz was besieged and captured, many of its citizens were exiled, and the art of printing was introduced into many European cities.

Throughout the remainder of the century the Bible in Latin continued to be printed in frequent and splendid editions. Mr. Stevens says that during the first forty years of printing, the Bible exceeded in amount all other books put together, and that "its quality, style and variety were not a whit behind its quantity." Not less than a thousand editions of the Bible were printed before the end of the century, most of them of the largest and costliest kind, and nearly all of them in Latin. During this period Bibles were printed also in German, Italian, and other modern languages, but these will not be considered until after this brief sketch of the best known Latin Bibles which followed the first four that have been described.

The EGGESTEYN BIBLES are usually catalogued as the *fifth*, *sixth* and *seventh* Latin Bibles, and attributed to *Heinrich Eggesteyn, Strasburg*, 1468, '69, '70. For a time he was a partner of Mentelin, the printer of the Third Latin and First German Bible, and was himself the printer of the Second German Bible. Eggesteyn published many other large folios. He was a man of considerable prominence, being a master of arts and philosophy, an officer of the city, and the chancellor of the Bishop at Strasburg.

Two of Eggesteyn's Latin Bibles were in the Caxton Exhibition, both from the Althorp Library, lent by Earl Spencer, one entered as the First Edition, 1468, (?) the other as " 1469, (?) sometimes attributed to J. Baemler, of Augsburg, but the type the same as that generally attributed to Eggesteyn, and the paper-mark undoubtedly his."

Three of Eggesteyn's Bibles are on exhibition in the Lenox Library, one marked " 1468–70, (?) the fifth Latin Bible," another marked " 1470, (?) " and another marked "Eggesteyn's second edition, Duke of Sussex Copy, The Seventh Latin Bible."

The ZELL BIBLES bring us to Cologne, the third city to receive the art of printing from Mentz, where *Ulric Zell*, probably a workman of Schoffer, is believed to have printed two folio editions of the Latin Bible, 1470 and 1471. The first book with a date, known to have been printed at Cologne, is *St. Chrysostom on the Fiftieth Psalm*, 1466. It is attributed to Zell, whose name is of special interest to us, because he has been mentioned as the chief instructor of William Caxton, the first English printer. Mr. Blades, who has written most exhaustively in regard to Caxton, does not admit this, though he recognizes the fact that Caxton was in Cologne during his residence on the Continent. He attributes Caxton's typographical work entirely to his association with Colard Mansion at Bruges or elsewhere. Two of Zell's Cologne Bibles were in the Caxton Exhibition, one from the Althorp and the other from the Bodleian Library. Though Zell's first dated book was printed in 1466, some bibliographers believe that he began to print as early as 1462. He was not only one of the earliest printers, but one who introduced improvements. After 1467 he always spaced out the lines of his books to an even length. Mr. Blades argues from this that Mansion and Caxton did not learn their art from him, or they would have made use of this improvement in their first productions.

By this time Italy, Bohemia, Switzerland and France had printing-presses, Italy being the first to receive the art from Germany.

The SWEYNHEYM AND PANNARTZ BIBLE, printed at Rome, 1471, *is the first Bible printed out of Germany.* In the same year two different translations into Italian were printed at Venice.

Arnold Pannartz and Conrad Sweynheym were Germans, probably workmen of Gutenberg and Fust. They were invited and welcomed to Subiaco, near Rome, by Cardinal Torquemada, the head of the Benedictine monastery, in which they established their press. Leading ecclesiastical officials gave them encouragement and help, not dreaming that this magic art would in a few generations completely destroy their temporal power and vastly impair their spiritual supremacy. Sweynheym and Pannartz's first known work, *Cicero de Oratore*, is believed to have been printed at Subiaco in 1465.

In 1467 they had removed to Rome, where they were established in the house and under the protection of Prince Massimo, and published over eight volumes a year for five years, producing 12,000 copies of books before 1474. Their works were mainly editions of classic authors, and were not so profitable as the large theological folios by which Mentelin, of Strasburg, had been enriched. There is a letter extant in which these printers appeal to Pope Sixtus IV. for help, giving a list of their works. Sweynheym retired from the firm and devoted himself to copper-plate engraving. Their last dated book was issued in December, 1473, though Pannartz continued to print for a few years. Both are said to have died before 1477.

This Roman Latin Bible, 1471, contains the name of the printers and the place and date, being the Second Bible with a date. Only 275 copies were printed.

The wonderful Althorp or Spencer Library furnished

the copy in the Caxton Exhibition.   This Library is one
of the richest in the world in specimens illustrating the
early history of typography, and especially the early
history of the printed Bible.   In this latter respect it is
surpassed by the Lenox Library, of which Mr. Stevens
says : " The collection of Bibles and parts thereof in the
Lenox Library of New York, in all languages, is probably
unsurpassed in rare and valuable editions, especially in
the English language, by any library, public or private."

CHAPTER XI.

✳

𝕷𝖆𝖙𝖎𝖓 𝕭𝖎𝖇𝖑𝖊𝖘.

BASLE AND NUREMBERG: 1471–1480.

IN MAKING THIS RECORD of Fifteenth Century Latin Bibles we have journeyed from Mentz to Strasburg, Cologne and Rome, where Sweynheym and Pannartz printed their Bible in 1471. There is a *Latin Bible by Schoffer, Mentz*, 1472, which very closely resembles that of 1462, but these Bibles are not identical.

Switzerland was the next country after Italy to receive printing from Germany. Bohemia received it about the same time, and the third place in this respect is given to it by Mr. Hawkins. But the next Bibles on record are attributed to Basle. In the Caxton Exhibition there were three different folio Latin Bibles which may be called The RODT AND RICHEL BIBLES, as they are attributed to Berthold Rodt and Bernard

Richel, of Basle, Switzerland.   They are all without
names and dates, their origin being inferred from the
type used, and other indications.   In the Catalogue they
are entered as follows :

> The one with 436 leaves, Rodt and Richel, 1473 (?).
>
> The one with 537 leaves, Rodt, 1474 (?).
>
> The one with 460 leaves, Richel, 1474 (?).

The Rodt and Richel Bible on exhibition in the
Lenox Library corresponds with the first of these, having
436 leaves in the two volumes.

Berthold Rodt, called also Berthold Ruppel de
Hanau, was a witness in the famous law suit between
Gutenberg and Fust at Mentz.   When these Bibles were
printed at Basle, the city was not yet a member of the
Swiss confederation, but being Swiss in spirit, and about
to be so in fact, it is considered as belonging to that
country in this connection.

Very erroneous notions prevail as to the money value
of old Bibles, because large prices are paid for certain
rare and interesting copies.   It is only less remarkable
to observe how small a price is asked for other examples
of very early printing.   In the catalogue of a London
bookseller recently received, there is a Latin Bible,
entered as "in the types of Rodt and Richel, Basle,
about 1470, 2 vols., folio, very fine copy, tall and clean,
half vellum, with ties, £5, 15s. 6d."   It ought to modify
the expectations of those who have old books to sell, to
know that beautiful and perfect volumes, Bibles and

other books, genuine *incunabula*, printed by famous printers during the first half century of printing, can be bought in London and New York for ten, twenty or thirty dollars each, and often for much less.

Other BASLE BIBLES. This city has the distinction of being the first city to produce the *Bible in octavo*, that is, a Bible of the size of the vast majority of books now printed for ordinary reading. This Bible has consequently been called the first edition of the "poor man's Bible." The "poor man" in this connection must mean the poor scholar, for poor men in that day could not read in their own tongue, much less in Latin. It was doubtless very welcome to poor students and ecclesiastics. This Latin Bible was printed by *John Froben de Hammelbruck at Basle* 1491, and is one of his first books, if not the first. The splendidly bound and illuminated copy of this Bible in the Bodleian Library does not look like a "poor man's Bible." Froben printed a quarto Latin Bible in 1495, and a folio Latin Bible in 1498.

His name is inseparably associated with that of *Erasmus*, the greatest scholar and man of letters of his day. Soon after the beginning of the next century Erasmus settled permanently in Basle, and became Froben's editor and literary adviser. This association resulted in making Basle for the time the great literary centre of Europe, and Froben's press the most celebrated. His New Testaments in Greek and Latin, and other works, belong to a later period.

In this same year there was also a *folio Latin Bible by Nicolas Keslers, Basle,* 1491.

After 1474 great Bibles were multiplied in both Latin and German. Among the most famous of these were The COBURGER BIBLES, the first of which was *the folio Latin Bible, printed by Anthony Coburger at Nuremberg,* 1475. He is said to have had twenty-four presses and one hundred men employed daily, besides furnishing work to printers at Basle, Lyons, and other places. Coburger printed thirteen editions of the Bible in twenty-six years, twelve in Latin and one in German, all large and handsome folios. Copies of his Latin Bibles were in the Caxton Exhibition dated 1475, 1477, 1478, 1479, 1480. His Latin Bibles of 1477 and 1480 are on exhibition at the Lenox Library. The broad margins of the 1477 copy are completely covered with commentaries, emendations and interlineations in the handwriting of Philip Melancthon.

Some time ago I saw a copy of the 1477 Coburger Bible for sale at the rooms of the Presbyterian Board of Publication in Philadelphia, where it had been placed by the owner, who was waiting for an offer. A copy of this same Bible is thus entered in a bookseller's catalogue recently sent from London :

Biblia Sacra Latina. 2 vols. in 1, folio; in the original oak boards, covered with stamped pigskin, very rare, £30. In regia civitate, Nurnbergn. p. Antonium Coburger, 1477.

"A remarkably fine, clean and large copy, a number

of the leaves having rough, uncut edges. The end leaves bear the water-marks of the Bull's Head and the Arms of John the Fearless. Laing's sold in 1879 for £84. The present copy contains a bookseller's description of one priced £100."

Other NUREMBERG BIBLES. Nuremberg produced another great folio Latin Bible in the same year in which Coburger printed his first edition. It was printed by *A. Frisner and J. Sensenschmid, Nuremberg*, 1475.

The first book printed at Nuremberg with a date is Franciscus de Retza's *Comestiorium Vitiorum*, 1470, and is attributed to Sensenschmid and Keffer. Sensenschmid is said to have been a man of wealth. He associated himself with Henry Keffer, a workman of Gutenberg, who appeared as a witness in the law suit with Fust. Keffer is supposed to have established himself as a printer in Nuremberg as early as 1469. Mr. Hawkins attributes to Keffer and Sensenschmid a book printed at Nuremberg in 1470, according to its colophon. But Nuremberg became famous in the history of printing from the extraordinary enterprise of Coburger. He was the publisher of that large and entertaining volume, *The Nuremberg Chronicle*, 1493, containing more than two thousand impressions from wood-cuts, being a summary of history, geography and general information, edited or compiled by Hartman Schedel. It is a royal folio, and is sold for more or less than $200, according to the size and condition of the copy. A London bookseller's catalogue, recently received, offers a very tall copy, 18½

inches by 12¼, beautifully bound in morocco super
extra, by Riviére, for £35.   It is said that there were
seventeen master type printers and many block-book
printers in Nuremberg before 1500.   It was just at this
period, at the end of the 15th and the beginning of the
16th century, that Albert Durer began to make his art,
himself and Nuremberg illustrious.   It was the Bible
which made him, as well as Wiclif, a morning star of the
Reformation.

CHAPTER XII.

❉

Latin Bibles.

PLACENTIA OR PIACENZA, ITALY, is credited with *the first Bible printed in Quarto.* It is a Latin Bible printed by *Johannes Petrus d'Ferratis, Placentia,* 1475. Copies of this Bible are in the Ambrosian Library at Milan, and the Althorp Library, England.

In the Caxton Exhibition there was *a folio Latin Bible attributed to Strasburg,* 1475, with no name of printer, lent by Dr. Ginsburg. His collection of Bibles numbers two or three thousand editions, including many of the earliest and rarest in different languages.

The year 1476 was a remarkable year for splendid folio editions of the Bible in Latin. No less than five are well known, one of which, by Sensenschmid, has already been mentioned in connection with Nuremberg.

Another of these folios brings us to France, the next great country after Germany and Italy, to receive the Art of Printing.   Guillaume Fichet and Jean de la Pierre, members of the Sorbonne, induced three German printers, Ulric Gering, Martinus Crantz and Michael Friburger, to come to Paris, where they fitted up a room for them in the Sorbonne, in which they began to print in 1470.   There is a copy of their Bible in the Lenox Library, which is described as by *Gering, Crantz and Friburger* (1476 ?), *folio.   The first Bible printed at Paris.*   Panzer says that there were 85 printers and 790 works printed in Paris during the fifteenth century.

Another folio Latin Bible printed in this year brings us to Naples, where printing was introduced by Sixtus Riessinger, a priest of Strasburg, in 1471.   Florence, Bologna, Ferrara, and many other Italian cities received it about the same time.   Matt. Moravus printed at Genoa with Michael de Monacho in 1474.   He removed the next year to Naples, and in the year following printed his *folio Latin Bible*, a copy of which is in the Lenox Library, entered as : By *Matt. Moravus, Naples,* 1476.

Two other Latin Bibles of this date were printed at Venice, and will be considered later.   In this year an edition of the *Aurea Biblia*, was printed by *Johan Zeiner de Reutlingen, at Ulm,* 1476.   This is a manual of Bible Histories by *Ant. Rampigollis*, which had been previously printed in one dated and several undated editions.

VENICE occupies a proud position in the early history

of printing, both for the amount and excellence of her work. Even among the unlearned the names of some of her great printers are better known than the names of her wealthiest merchants or most magnificent rulers. It is estimated that Venice produced 2,000,000 of volumes during the first half century of printing. This may lessen our wonder that nearly every lover of old books in Europe or America has in his library more than one book over four hundred years old. Before 1500, Venice had had more than two hundred printers, who had printed about 3,000 editions, including Venetian Bibles, to the extent of twenty editions.

Her first printer was *John de Spira*, supposed to have been of Spire on the Rhine. His first dated work is *Cicero's Epistolæ ad Familiares*, 1468, a folio of 125 leaves.

Two translations of the Bible into Italian were printed at Venice in 1471, one by Vindelin, brother of John de Spira, the other by N. Jenson. But *the first Latin Bible printed at Venice*, is the *small folio by F. de Hailbrun and N. de Frankfordia*, 1475. *Hailbrun* printed a *Latin Bible in Quarto*, 1480.

In the next year two folio Latin Bibles appeared at Venice : one by these same printers, *F. de Hailbrun and N. de Frankfordia*, 1476; the other by *Nicolas Jenson*, 1476. There is a copy of this 1476 Jenson Bible at the Lenox Library, in the same case with three other Latin Bibles of the same date, all of which have just been mentioned.

Jenson is pre-eminent among printers of the fifteenth century for the perfection of his work, his skill as an engraver enabling him to surpass his rivals in many respects. He had been employed at the mint in Paris, and was sent by Charles VII. in 1458 to Mentz to learn the new art from Gutenberg. Louis XI. did not encourage his father's project, and Jenson was unable to establish a press at Paris. He removed to Venice, where his books in improved Roman type soon made him famous. He received a title from Pope Sixtus IV., and died in 1482. Mr. De Vinne says: "As a type-founder, printer and ink-maker, Jenson had no rival, and left no proper successor." *Another folio Latin Bible* by *Jenson*, *Venice*, 1479, was in the Caxton Exhibition, lent by the British and Foreign Bible Society. There were *two folio Latin Bibles* in the previous year, by different printers, one by *Leonardus Vuild de Ratisbon and N. de Frankfordia*, *Venice*, 1478, the other by *T. de Reynsburck and Reynaldi de Novimagio*, *Venice*, 1478. Among the numerous Bibles of the closing years of the century were a Latin *folio*, *by Herbort de Siligenstat*, *Venice*, 1483, and another *Latin folio by Paganinus de Paganinis*, *Venice*, 1495.

Two Quarto Bibles have been mentioned in this connection. Another *Quarto Latin Bible*, *by Georgius Ravabenis*, *Venice*, 1487, is *the first Bible with a separate title-page*. There were *Quarto Latin Bibles* by *Simon Bevilaqua*, *Venice*, 1494 and 1498.

The *Latin Bible*, by *Hieronimus de Paganinis*, *Venice*,

1492, is *the earliest Bible with an illustration on the title-page.* There is a *Latin Bible, Octavo,* by the same printer, 1497.

HEBREW AND GREEK. *The first complete edition of the Bible in Hebrew* was printed at *Soncino by Abraham ben Chayin de' Tintori,* 1488, *folio.* The Pentateuch had been printed by the same printer at Bologna in 1482, and other portions of the Old Testament later.

The Psalms were printed in Greek and Latin at Milan, 1481.

The great editions of the Bible in Greek belong to the sixteenth century.

CHAPTER XIII.

❋

Vernacular Bibles.

FIFTEENTH CENTURY.

IT IS NOT KNOWN at what time the Bible was translated into the German, though fragments of such translations have come down from comparatively early times. There must have been a German translation early in the fifteenth century, for about ten years after the invention of printing, the First German Bible was printed at Strasburg about 1466, by Johannes Mentelin, the printer of The Third Latin Bible. It is a folio, containing 405 leaves, printed in double columns, 60 lines to a column. Two copies of this Bible were in the Caxton Exhibition, one lent by the Queen, the other by Earl Spencer. Both are richly illuminated in gold and colors, but in entirely different styles. The size and richness of the book indicate that it was not designed for popular reading. The Second German Bible is also a folio. It is attributed to Heinrich Eggesteyn, Strasburg, 1466, and, like the preceding, has 405 leaves, printed in double columns, 60 lines to a column.

These earliest Bibles in German were followed by twelve more editions in High German and three in Low German, all printed before Luther issued his New Testament in 1522. Do these editions discredit the familiar statement that Luther gave to the people the Bible in the vernacular? Not in the least. For all these fourteen editions in High German and three editions in Low German are known, classed, and described by bibliographers as *important*, *splendid*, *sumptuous*. In this respect they were like the numerous Latin Bibles of the fifteenth century, some of which we have enumerated and described. Even now, when learning and wealth are widely distributed among the masses, it would not be possible to give the Bible to any nation, if it were printed only in magnificent Library editions. No book of any kind ever became a people's book which was not printed in an inexpensive form. No other books compete with the Bible, the "Imitation of Christ," and Bunyan's "Pilgrim's Progress," and no other books have been issued in so vast a number of cheap editions. Let us bear this in mind in enumerating the expensive folio German Bibles which preceded the translations of Luther. They are thus recorded, beginning with the two already mentioned:

(1.) Johannes Mentelin, Strasburg, *circa* 1464–66.

(2.) Heinrich Eggesteyn, Strasburg, *circa* 1466.

(3.) Jodocus Pflanzmann, Augsburg, *circa* 1470–73.

(4.) Frisner and Sensenschmid, Nürnburg, *circa* 1470–73.

(5.) Günter Zeiner, Augsburg, *circa* 1473–75.

(6.) Günter Zeiner, Augsburg, dated 1477.

(7.) Anton Sorg, Augsburg, 1477.

(8.) Anton Sorg, Augsburg, 1480.

(9.) Anton Coburger, Nürnburg, 1483.

(10.) Johann Gruninger, Strasburg, 1485.

(11.) Hans Schönsperger, Augsburg, 1487.

(12.) Hans Schönsperger, Strasburg, 1490.

(13.) Hans Otmar, Augsburg, 1507.

(14.) Silvan Otmar, Augsburg, 1518.

Besides these splendid editions in High German, there were three equally grand editions published in Low German :

(1.) Quentel, Cologne, 1480.

(2.) Stephan Arndes, Lübeck, 1494.

(3.) Halberstadt, 1522.

Of these Bibles eight are in the British Museum. Dr. Ginsburgh is said to have all the fourteen in High German. A beautiful copy of the Eggesteyn Bible is in the Lenox Library. One of the Augsburg 1477 Bibles is the first German Bible with a date.

Italy comes next to Germany in obtaining the Scriptures printed in a native tongue. Two translations were issued in 1471. Both were printed at Venice, one by Vindelin de Spira, the other by Nicolas Jenson, the best printer of the fifteenth century. Earl Spencer's copy of the Italian Bible, printed by N. Jenson, at Venice, 1471, was in the Caxton Exhibition. Like the other Bibles of the period, it is a folio 16¼ by 11 inches, without title-page, pagination or signatures, fifty lines to a full page. Its date in Roman letters is at the end of the New Testament. An Italian Bible, with the history of the Septuagint by Aristeas, translated into Italian by N. de Malermi, was printed in Venice, 1477, by Antonio Bolognese. It is a folio in two parts. Another folio Italian Bible was printed at Venice by Joan Rosso Vercellese, 1487.

France furnished still less of the Bible in the vernacular during this period. There was a New Testament in French, quarto, printed by Buyer, at Lyons, in about 1477. There was a Bible in French paraphrase printed about 1487.

Even the Dutch language does not furnish much more than this. Mr. Hawkins mentions the Bible in Dutch as the first book printed at Delft, 1477, by Jacob Jacobs Zoen and Mauritius Temants Zoen. It is in two volumes, folio.

Bohemia produced a Bible in 1488, a folio, printed at Prague. Mr. Hawkins mentions another Bohemian Bible, as one of the very rarest of early Bibles, a folio, printed at Kuttenberg, 1489.

Though this is not given as a complete record of ante-reformation translations of the Scriptures, it includes the best known editions of the Bible in continental tongues printed in the first half century of the art.

During this period there was no Bible printed in English. So great is our poverty in this respect, that in the technical sense there are no old English Bibles — none that is included in the class of books called *incunabula*. All that can be said is that early English printing is not actually destitute of all traces of the Scriptures. William Caxton, our first English printer, whose life and work were very obscurely known until our own day, printed in 1483, the first year of the reign of Richard III., a folio called *The Golden Legende*. This contains an English translation of nearly all the Pentateuch and the Gospels. How much it was read we do not know, but it was the forerunner of Tyndale and Coverdale, preparing the way for the Reformation. In Gen. iii., 7, it reads: "𝕬𝖓𝖉 𝖙𝖍𝖚𝖘 𝖙𝖍𝖊𝖞 𝖐𝖓𝖊𝖜𝖊 𝖙𝖍𝖆𝖙 𝖙𝖍𝖊𝖞 𝖜𝖊𝖗𝖊 𝖓𝖆𝖐𝖊𝖉. 𝕬𝖓𝖉 𝖙𝖍𝖊𝖞 𝖙𝖔𝖐𝖊 𝖋𝖎𝖌𝖌𝖊 𝖑𝖊𝖚𝖎𝖘 𝖆𝖓𝖉 𝖘𝖊𝖜𝖊𝖉 𝖙𝖍𝖊𝖒 𝖙𝖔𝖌𝖞𝖉𝖊𝖗 𝖋𝖔𝖗 𝖙𝖔 𝖈𝖔𝖚𝖊𝖗𝖊 𝖙𝖍𝖊𝖞𝖗 𝖒𝖊𝖒𝖇𝖗𝖊𝖘 𝖎𝖓 𝖒𝖆𝖓𝖊𝖗 𝖔𝖋 𝖇𝖗𝖊𝖈𝖍𝖎𝖘." This anticipates the reading of the famous "Breeches Bible," which is the Genevan Version of 1560.

All that bibliographical students have discovered in regard to early Vernacular Bibles confirms the statement that before the Reformation they were comparatively unknown. They were not printed in any country, in a way that would bring them within the reach of large numbers. Perhaps it would have been impossible to do this, there were so few who knew how to read.

Not until the second quarter of the following century were those German and English versions of the Bible printed which have moulded the language, literature and life of these great peoples. All these earliest Bibles, Latin and Vernacular, which have been mentioned in this volume, are of interest chiefly on account of their connection with the history of the art of printing. Those who appreciate books as historic objects, and especially those who cherish ancient Bibles, may find something that interests them in this study in bibliography.

Printed at the Printing
House of E. R. Cole
1 William St.
New York
* *
*
MDCCCLXXXVIII.

Index.